Loretta P. Smith-Johnson
Shekinah Glory Christian Chu
17 Alexander Street
Newark, New Jersey 07106
www.Carmiministries.com

MW00945559

"Drink Deeply"
By Loretta P. Smith-Johnson

Printed in the USA

ISBN 10 1517637279
ISBN 13 9781517637279

Scripture quotations are taken from:

AMP   Amplified Bible (1965)
ESV   English Standard Version (2001)
KJV   King James Version (1611) (1769)
NASB New American Standard Bible (1971) (1995)
NIV   New International Version (1984)
NLT[1]   New Living Translation (1st ed. 1996; 2nd ed. 2004)
NKJV New King James Version (1982) (1990)
NRSV New Revised Standard Version (1989)

Cover design by **VerySmartGrafix@gmail.com**

"For I know the plans I have for you, declares the Lord, plans for welfare and not for evil, to give you a future and a hope. Then you will call upon me and come and pray to me, and I will hear you. You will seek me and find me, when you seek me with all your heart."

Jeremiah 29:11-13 ESV

ACKNOWLEGEMENTS

From the depths of my heart, "thank you" to:

- My Lord and Savior, **Jesus Christ**, the Author and Finisher of my faith and Giver of New Life. "For in him dwelleth all the fullness of the Godhead bodily. And ye are complete in him, which is the head of all principality and power;" (Col. 2:9-10)

- My dear husband, **Pastor Alexis Johnson**, who always encourages me to take on the "hard things", because God is Faithful and Able. Thank you for loving me.

- My children, **Bianca, Nahor, Emmanuel, and Micah**, for always believing in me. I love you all, dearly.

- My special daughter, **Jackie,** who is shouting in heaven.

- My big sister, confidant and friend, **Mary**, aka Auntie Ease, who called every day to remind me to write AND earned my early degrees with me…. thanks forever…I love you.

- My Shekinah Glory Church family, my Safe House and Women Live on the Line families, and all those that have encouraged me by allowing me to minister to them, I do not know how I would survive without your love, support and open spirit to download what God gives me.

- My wonderful, talented, long-suffering, patient, anointed, and reliable administrator, editor, graphic artist, critic, sister and friend "at all times", Deacon **Viveca Y. Stamper**. Thanks for everything…everything.

PREFACE

As I made my way through the readings printed here, I noticed a recurring theme: the new life that is available in God. I realized after further introspection, that this has also been a recurring theme in my life, and ministry. What a revelation! It is most intriguing because I did not set out to write a book, but to just record my thoughts on various passages of scripture as I studied them for sermons, teachings, presentations, and assignments.

As I continue to reflect on this admission, I am challenged to do just what I am asking of my readers: reflect in writing. It has been my experience, that when I deliberately get in touch with my thoughts, some wonderful ideas and creative responses are unearthed.

Immediate recording of these thoughts is essential, for in just moments, they are gone, almost forgotten forever, replaced by matters of urgency. But, as I have learned, I challenge you to be diligent to write your ideas, dreams, visions, musings, aspirations, hopes, goals, ambitions, and wishes. They may seem far-fetched, incredible, and difficult, but with God nothing is impossible. One word of caution, though, be sure that you seek instruction and timing from God before you begin to pursue it. You'll get clear answers sometimes and then at other times, you might not hear anything conclusive. (Do I have a witness?)

I have included some questions and prompts to help you respond immediately after reading the selection, but you can be creative and do whatever comes to mind. Just make sure you respond; God wants to say something through you, just like He is saying something through me. Maybe that will be the start of your book!!! (He that hath an ear....)

It would be great if you were able to recognize a recurring theme that resonates in your writings. But if you don't want to get that serious, just enjoy a daily treat that will refresh you and thrust you forward into your destiny.

May God's most radical thoughts and dreams overtake you as you read and envision; grow and are encouraged; create and implement what has never been seen, simply because you dared to believe God!

+LPSJ

INTRODUCTION

One of my favorite pastimes is sitting with friends and a good cup of coffee. There's nothing like it. Or maybe for you it is a hot cup of tea. Whether you are a tea drinker or a "Java Jane", there is just something so soothing about a good hot cup of your preferred drink. The atmosphere changes when hazelnut coffee mates with hazelnut creamer, especially within the company of friends and family. And please don't add a piece of apple cake or a lemon scone, wow, there are just no words that can adequately describe the feeling of euphoria that comes upon the coffee lover at the mere thought!!!!

So it is with a good thought, idea, vision, dream or musing that comes from God concerning His Word. In whatever way you can make that word practical, do it...whatever it takes to make the word work, pursue it. The practicality of the Word will soothe even the most bothersome situation.

My intention here is to share thoughts around the Word in ways that will cause you to drink and to be soothed by it, to be refreshed, to have that moment in time altered by the reality of it. Just like a cup of coffee just seems to make everything okay, so it is with the Word of God made practical. Understanding and being able to convert the truth of the Word into the practical reality of your life is better than a cup of hazelnut coffee with hazelnut creamer just before bed.

My prayer for you is that these writings, musings and ideas will refresh and bring comfort, challenging you to think deeply and intimately into the Word so that it comes alive and cultivates a belief system that affects behaviors. This will move you into a new dimension. That dimension is an existence that is characterized by a certain set of beliefs and behaviors that produce an intentional outcome. Go ahead live in this next dimension by drinking deeply, daily. Join me in this wonderful exercise by writing your thoughts on the pages provided.

I consider you partners in ministry. For without your loyalty and readership, DrinkDeeply would not make sense. Thank you for your thirst for the Word and for encouraging this servant to inquire of the Lord and to deliver what God is saying at a time when many have no desire to hear. Thank you also for referring DrinkDeeply to your family and friends and for using the daily words as a ministry tool of witness, encouragement, and conversation to glorify God. Be blessed as we go forth.

I want to encourage you to intentionally increase your love for the Word and for the Will of God. We must know what God is saying so that we can know what God has called us to do in these next seasons. We are committed to hearing from God, to communicating God's Will, and to encouraging and supporting you in your everyday life and ministry to the end that the Kingdom of God is established in the earth realm.

Our faithful God has been shifting and affecting fresh revelation for this next season. So, DrinkDeeply! Be blessed and keep me in your prayers, as you are in mine.

New Models and New Mentors

Of course we think we know it all. Even the most spiritually mature of us, at some point and in some way, think we know it all. But this is a season of new models and new mentors. Be careful not to ignore the new ideas and the new thoughts that are confronting you in this hour, for God is presenting you with alternative approaches to the things you must deal with (that perhaps are not the most pleasant) and new ways to accomplish and realize His perfected will in your life.

Please do not ignore the instructions that are coming in new ways, through new people, new ideas and new thoughts. You've never had these ideas before. You've never thought this way before. You are absolutely right, and that is exactly why they are most necessary now. That which you've never had and the places that you've never been will be birthed out of the "new" that God presents, and you will find yourself right where He wants you to be.

So receive the new models and receive the new mentors by adjusting your life so that they have room to establish God's intentions in your mind, in your body, in your spirit, in your affairs, in your everyday life—in you.

"Yes, I will tell you of things that are entirely new, things you never heard of before..." Isaiah 48:8a (NLT)

Your Reflections

What are some of the new thoughts you've had recently and what have you done with them?

A Breakthrough

So you need a breakthrough—most of us do. In some area or another, there is a place of stuck that needs to be broken up so that the power of the Living God may flow freely in that area.

Breakthroughs only come by believing that they can come—not by believing that the possibility exists, but that the breakthrough really can happen. Breakthroughs are simply believing God for the impossible. If we can believe God for the possible, then we can just as assuredly believe Him for the impossible. The difference between the possible and impossible in our lives is the moment we believe God can do it—not that it can happen—but that God can do it.

I believe that God is able to all things. According to His Word, God said that there is nothing too hard for Him to do. That means ALL that we have the capacity to ever imagine He can do. The issue is whether or not we believe He will.

I choose to believe that every hard place in my life is a place that God can smooth out and make workable and easy—and that's where the breakthrough comes. It comes because I believe God is able and that He will. Make a decision to believe God for your breakthrough today.

"Jesus said to him, "If you can believe, all things are possible to him who believes." Mark 9:23 (NKJV)

Your Reflections

A breakthrough in my life would be:

A Great Time of Opportunity, Change & Possibility

This is a season of great revelation and a season of possibility through receiving revelation. If you will just hear what God is saying, your life will be totally and completely changed.

I'm going to call it a 'Sponge Bob' season where everything you hear, you are able to receive. You are able to absorb and to suck it into every part of your life. You are now able to receive the truth through revelation knowledge spiritually, mentally, and emotionally — and it will affect your life in every way.

This is such a great time of opportunity. This is such a great time for change. This is such a great time for all that is possible to become reality. God is in the business of blessing, of giving, and it is His intention to bring full and complete revelation with understanding to all His people.

This is the time for God's purpose, so receive afresh and anew.

"To everything there is a season, A time for every purpose under heaven:" Ecclesiastes 3:1 (NKJV)

Your Reflections

Some of the things that God is revealing to me are:

You Too, Shall Be Whole

I AM the God that healeth thee. I AM the Lord your healer. I sent My Word and I healed your disease. I AM the Lord your healer.

I still heal, and because of My wholeness, you too shall be whole. I heal you. I heal you of physical disorder. I heal you of physical disease. I heal you of physical misalignment. I heal you. I heal you of mental and emotional issues. My healing is complete. I know you do not believe that I still heal, but I do. My healing is the children's bread. My healing restores and re-establishes intended purpose. And I heal because I have purpose for your life!

So, HANDS BE HEALED; HEARTS BE HEALED; MINDS BE HEALED; RELATIONSHIPS BE HEALED! For I AM the Lord, thy Healer. [Thus Saith The Lord, Our God.]

"Then she came and worshiped Him, saying, "Lord, help me!" But He answered and said, "It is not good to take the children's bread and throw it to the little dogs." And she said, "Yes, Lord, yet even the little dogs eat the crumbs which fall from their masters' table." Then Jesus answered and said to her, "O woman, great is your faith! Let it be to you as you desire." And her daughter was healed from that very hour." Matthew 15:25-28 (NKJV)

Your Reflections

Father God, please flow your healing power to the following areas of my life:

New Heights & New Sights

You're reaching new heights because you're doing what you've never done before. You're realizing new gains and attaining new strength, all because finally you have chosen to believe Me — for real.

You're seeing new sights. Your vision is clearer. You're hearing My voice as you have never heard Me before, and you're experiencing My Glory like you've only ever dreamed in times past. Yes, it is really happening, and it is because you really believe Me for the first time in a long time.

Don't try to figure Me out. Come into agreement with Me. I AM causing streams to flow. I AM causing rivers to be unleashed. I AM causing doors to close. I AM causing opportunities to open. I AM causing distractions to shrink and to wither away. The ability to focus shall be increased. I WILL speak in ways that you have not heard. I WILL say things that you have only imagined. This I do because of My Love for you.

Yes, I AM still God and I still do what I do best — and that is, BEING GOD. I AM GOD and the impossible is possible with Me — if you believe. [Thus Says the Lord, Our God]

"Jesus asked the boy's father, 'How long has he been like this? From childhood,' he answered. 'It has often thrown him into fire or water to kill him. But if you can do anything, take pity on us and help us. If you can?' said Jesus. 'Everything is possible for him who believes.' Immediately the boy's fathers exclaimed, 'I do believe; help me overcome my unbelief!'" Mark 9:21-24 (NIV)

Your Reflections

Yes, Lord. I hear you saying:

Isn't Peace Enough?

Peace, I leave you. My peace, I give to you; not as the world gives do I give to you. John 12:17

This great gift of peace that is given unto believers by God is being severely threatened by a pervasive atmosphere of drama. What a shame that we have to fight for the gift that was given to us, but I want to encourage you that it is oh so worth it! God gave us peace as a sign of our connection to Him, our attachment to Him, and our detachment to the world. The presence of peace in our lives is a sign that we belong to God. So, with everything within us, we must resist the opportunity to participate in drama at any level. Our continued participation is a sign and a demonstration that we are not connected to God.

Many of us are so familiar and used to participating in drama that "drama" is like our middle name. It seems that if we are not participating in some level of drama (confusion, discord, dissension, or dispute) we wonder, "What's wrong?" It is really sad that when things are 'too peaceful' we look around and wonder (become suspect of) what is going on. But understand this: Since God called Himself a God of Peace and says that He Himself is Jehovah Shalom, Our Peace, and then both of the meanings of Peace are appropriate signs of God's preeminence, prevalence and pervasiveness in our lives.

The Greek translation/definition of Peace is the presence of all things necessary. That is to say that there is NO loss, there is NO absence, and therefore, there is NO void. Whereas, drama and confusion create a casual attitude and notion that they are required (and sometimes even welcomed) in order to validate our lives.

Beloved, this is entirely inconsistent with and in spite of the reality that God, Himself, claims that HE IS PEACE and that THAT is enough of a validation that we have all things necessary with us.

So then, if we have all things necessary, then do we really need drama to validate our lives? Do we really need drama to indicate or identify who we are and what we can do? Isn't PEACE enough?

"You will keep him in perfect peace, Whose mind is stayed on You, Because he trusts in You." Isaiah 26:3 (NKJV)

Your Reflections

Draw an image of "peace".

Look At Yourself

This is not a season to be selfish or inward, but it is a season to be diligent about the business of building yourself up. This is not a season to be self-centered, but it is a season to be concerned about your self-growth and self-identity. In doing so, you present to others a stronger and more stable self (or 'you') that can be used by God to stabilize, to bring Good News, and to strengthen and encourage others.

We routinely occupy ourselves validating the anointing on the lives of others. Well, this is the time for us to see, to maintain, and to increase the anointing on our own lives through diligent self-examination and introspection. It is, many times, more difficult and a greater challenge to see areas of our own lives that need attention and correction. But trust me, once you identify (and accept) them as needing attention and as needing the power and anointing of God to call them in line, your yield will be the blessed assurance of knowing that our faithful God will do all that is necessary to bring them into perfect order. Just identify and acknowledge them. As soon as you say God, I need You to help me to have a greater measure of faith. He will bestow it upon you – just because you asked, and because you asked for His Glory. God sees this as an act of faith, and He will always respond accordingly.

Listen, we can always tell someone else what to do, but this is your time – this is your season. Come into agreement with what God wants for your life. Admit that you need it, and then let God do it.

"But let each one examine his own work, and then he will have rejoicing in himself alone, and not in another." Galatians 6:4 (NKJV)

Your Reflections

God, I could use some help in the following areas:

Sort Them Out

It's time sort things out and to relieve yourself of the plethora of ideas and thoughts that are constantly circling around in your mind. It's time to sort things out and to categorize the various ways that God is using to speak to you in this hour. It's time to gather your thoughts and begin to realize the benefit of understanding the categories of thoughts and ideas because that will help you gather your thoughts and to hear (in totality) what God is saying. Don't just think that the thoughts are just running wild without structure and without meaning. God is using thoughts to speak to you. For instance, if you start thinking of someone, then call, contact, or text the person. God has strategically dropped that person in your mind for a specific reason.

Just today, I was thinking of someone, called them, but was unable to make contact. Four hours later, I learned that at the very time that I'd called, that person was in great distress and needed to hear from someone who would direct their thoughts towards God. Even though I was unable to reach them, I thank God for the obedience that I was able to operate in. Even though the obedience did not yield what I thought it would, God still spoke to their heart and mind and they were ministered to mightily.

I can't help but think that we underestimate and don't give enough credence to the thoughts that God drops in our minds. They all have meaning and come to mind for reasons that we may not know or immediately discern, however they will most likely be revealed to us in the times to come.

So take the time to gather your thoughts. Take the time to gather your musings and ideas—for God is speaking to us and He does not speak to us in confusion. Rather, He causes us to be blessed by His decency and His order.

"Now all the earth sought the presence of Solomon to hear his wisdom, which God had put in his heart." 1 Kings 10:24 (NKJV) *"When I saw it, I considered it well; I looked on it and received instruction:"* Proverbs 24:32 (NKJV)

Your Reflections

My plan for greater wisdom in this area is:

Take Me Off Ignore

This word is to the seasoned saints. It is to those who know the voice of God and do not have to wonder whether or not they are hearing God—they know it.

Do not ignore God. Do not ignore what you know He is saying to you. You know you hear Him and you know He is speaking. You cannot ignore Him. Sure, you've been used to having things your way and you've been used to forcing things to come out your way (not being settled or in agreement until things are your way), but this time you have been positioned such that your only option is to listen (to hear) God—because what He is saying is for your good.

This is what God is trying to speak to your heart: Exchange your way for His way. It is not going to be easy, but it will be well worth it. In the end, His way will bring life, peace and joy. If you continue to try to advance or to continue in your own way, you will be forced to rewind and to repeat your efforts over and over again until you arrive at the place where you finally realize that you must do it God's way.

So, go ahead and do it God's way. Do it God's way and be satisfied that He, Who is God Alone, is well able to do all you desire Him to do. Yes, even those things you don't have the capacity or ability to fathom, He is willing to do. Yes, even those things to which you are not yet privy—He has already worked them out. The things you are trying to figure out, the things you are trying to solve, the things that give you pause, don't riddle God. He's already finished with them and moved on to the next thing.

Consider this: while you're still trying to figure out what you should even tell God to do, it is already in place. If you would just believe, your eyes would be opened and you would be able to see God's perfect will for your life—already worked out, already in operation, already done. But you must be obedient and willingly proceed because you want to.

Worship God and be at peace. Get God off ignore. Hear Him and be at peace.

"Now to Him who is able to do exceedingly abundantly above all that we ask or think, according to the power that works in us, to Him be glory in the church by Christ Jesus to all generations, forever and ever. Amen." Ephesians 3:20-21 (NKJV)

Your Reflections

God, forgive me for ignoring You when...

Make Your Lemonade

Some years ago, when I was about 15 years old, the walls and ceiling of my bedroom were covered with posters. It was a 'masterful display' of my pictures, saying, and mementos that reminded me of my favorite things. One particular poster was positioned very near my ceiling so that whenever I looked up from my bed, I could always see it. It read: "When Life Gives You Lemons, Make Lemonade".

I always wondered why I liked that saying. I used to think it was because I was an optimistic or positive thinker. But now I thoughtfully ascribe it to something more: It is the perspective that is necessary to achieve and operate in the world with a Kingdom mind-set—and therefore, with Kingdom victory. Furthermore, it is the posture of a value system that says: whatever is in me has the power to create something good out of something that is not so good. In this, it is not just a perspective, but a value system that causes us to understand that no matter what confronts us, our intrinsic value is such that we are able to change our situation because of our value—because of who we are in the image of God and what our purpose is in the Kingdom of God.

The value system necessary to succeed in the things of God has not so much (if anything) to do with what we can do, but more so with who we know made us and for what purposes we were made. This value system has everything to do with Whose Hands we are in, and because we value those Hands, we also value ourselves and our God-given ability to agree (line up) with the values of the Kingdom.

Indeed, life has given us lemons, but it takes good lemons to make good lemonade. Make your lemonade.

"Establishing and strengthening the souls and the hearts of the disciples, urging and warning and encouraging them to stand firm in the faith, and [telling them] that it is through many hardships and tribulations we must enter the kingdom of God." Acts 14:22 (AMP)

Your Reflections

I remember making good of a bad situation when...

100% Pure and Refreshing

Allow yourself to be dealt with by the Word of God. Allow the Word of God to be that refreshing bath that cleanses you from the disappointments, discouragements, pain, filth, guilt and shame inflicted upon you by the world, those that are in the world, and even those things that are self-inflicted. Allow the Word to refresh you. Allow the Word to wash you clean.

The Word of God is 100% pure—more pure than Ivory® could ever be. It is refreshing—more refreshing than Irish Springs® could ever be. It cleans deeper and is more thorough than any means, method or technique that we could ever develop.

Let the Word of God be a refreshing cleansing power in your life, for it is the Word of God that accomplishes the will of God. Anything else that makes an attempt at this assignment (like your own words, or words from others) may be too harsh, too acidic and too caustic to bring about a healthy wholeness (one that enables you to go on to the next issue).

Let the Word of God cleanse you—let it deal with you. Don't be afraid of the truth that comes from the Word of God. Because it IS truth and because it IS God, He knows how to use it in a way that does not cause condemnation, rejection, or increase guilt and shame. Rather, it allows us to deal with the reality of issues just as they are and to benefit from the compassion that the love of God employs. It really is the best, the most safe, and the greenest way to be cleansed.

Let the Word of God cleanse you, for in your refreshed state, you will be more apt to let the Word guide your next steps, your next set of emotions and the way you approach the next set of circumstances and challenges. It is SO important that at the onset—that is, the very moment you hear the Word of God—that you allow the Word of God to minister to you.

The very assignment of the Word of God that is presented to you and brought to your remembrance is so you can choose do deal with yourself according to the Word and not according to an anthology of actions or reactions derived from anything else. Allow yourself to be dealt with by the Word of God.

"For the word of God is living and powerful, and sharper than any two-edged sword, piercing even to the division of soul and spirit, and of joints and marrow..." Hebrews 4:12a (NKJV)

Your Reflections

I realized the power of the Word when....

I AM Shouting

I AM SHOUTING. I AM SHOUTING AND I AM TALKING VERY LOUDLY BECAUSE I WANT YOUR ATTENTION. My Voice is louder than every other voice around you, yet you continue to strain and to train your ear to hear every other voice, while refusing to hear Me. I HAVE "fixed it", however, so that you cannot ignore what I AM saying to you.

I AM SHOUTING in your left ear. I AM SHOUTING in your right ear. I AM SHOUTING. Even when you cover your ears, you will still hear Me, because I AM speaking to your spirit. I AM saying the things that you do not want to hear, but I AM saying them because I love you.

HEAR WHAT I AM SAYING TODAY. I will not be discouraged. I will not stop. I will not turn away. I will not be deterred. I love you and I will not allow you to have one moment without a bombardment of My love for you. I love you and I AM determined to pour out My love and even to push it on you. I AM not even upset when you don't "get it" – I AM more determined. I love you. [THUS SAITH THE LORD, OUR GOD]

"The LORD has appeared of old to me, saying:" Yes, I have loved you with an everlasting love; Therefore with lovingkindness I have drawn you." Jeremiah 31:3 (NKJV)
"...and is a discerner of the thoughts and intents of the heart." Hebrews 4:12b (NKJV)

Your Reflections

Right now I hear...

Not Undone

One of the most wonderful things about Our God is that He allows mistakes. Our foolishness doesn't undo Him. Our meltdowns don't undo Him. The things that undo us—even by the fact that we can be undone, don't undo Him. But in all those things He promised to never leave us and never forsake us.

So here we are melting down and God is standing right there. And here we are telling God what we think we know, but what He knows is far better than us. Yet, God is not offended nor is He moved to cause us to be cancelled out by those things. Instead, God extends mercy, He extends grace, He extends even His Hand to pull us up and remind us that He still loves us. The problem then is when we allow our own guilt to hinder us from the *full* benefit of a loving God. So we run and hide from Him—or at least we try.

In this season, we really need to begin to know the character of God and the ways of God and to benefit from them, instead of running from them. Let God's grace and forgiveness be a permanent feature in our lives from our standpoint—not just from His. This is so that we get the FULL benefit of being forgiven, really letting it work in our everyday lives, pointing us in the direction that He wants us to go—instead of something that we only shout and run around the church about.

God really does love us, and that's a very serious conclusion. He REALLY loves us. It is a love that we cannot explain; a love that shows up in SO many different ways; a love that is extravagant; a love that is exemplary; and a love with which we can love others.

"for the Father himself loves you, because you have loved me and have believed that I came from God." John 16: 27 (NRSV)

Your Reflections

Write a poem or some song lyrics that express your love for God.

Stop Mind Terrorism

There must be an all-out war against the hijacking of our thoughts, our musings and our minds. Mind terrorism occurs when 'a truth' is mishandled, misunderstood, or misdirected and thus, becomes re-routed to a place other than its intended destiny. For instance, the idea of naming it and claiming it; the idea that your thoughts create an atmosphere; the new-age idea of if you say it long enough, it will become. The roots of these ideas are principles that are found in the Word of God: calling those things which do not exist as though they did; as a man thinks in his heart, so is he; the power of life and death is in the tongue; etc.

The Bible is true, yet these biblical principles have been hijacked and mishandled as opportunities to create what we can control instead of demonstrating faith in that which is in line with the intended Will of God. These scriptures were intended to increase our faith in God, not to create atmospheres that we ourselves control. When we allow our thoughts concerning the Word of God to be hijacked and redirected away from the Kingdom of God to destinations that can only be referenced by flesh or that are primarily focused on self, then we are most assuredly victims of mind terrorism.

The issue is the destination. The issue is where we end up. Where do we want to end up? We want to end up with faith in God. We want to end up where God intended us to go. We want to end up on Kingdom Boulevard in Kingdom Land.

Therefore, we must come against and shut down every opportunity and every possibility of mind terrorism at every point. That is accomplished by insisting on intimacy with God. Anything that is not like Him (doesn't look like Him, doesn't sound like Him, doesn't smell like Him) has to be shut down so that God's will is done in our lives. Stop Mind Terrorism.

"And do not be conformed to this world, but be transformed by the renewing of your mind, that you may prove what is that good and acceptable and perfect will of God." Romans 12:2 (NKJV)

", casting down arguments and every high thing that exalts itself against the knowledge of God, bringing every thought into captivity to the obedience of Christ," 2 Corinthians 10:5 (NKJV)

Your Reflections

I am struggling with the idea...

What Were You Thinking?

I am in the process of hearing a Word from the Lord. It is an idea that is very difficult to grasp, yet it is so absolutely important. It is fundamental that we know and understand this: What we think is important to God. It is not just what we do that is important, but it is what we do coupled with what we think. What we think ultimately affects what we do; however what we do doesn't always indicate what we think.

The Bible clearly states that a double-minded man is unstable in all his ways. Well, my understanding of double-mindedness is not just saying one thing and doing another, but it is to think in a way that is inconsistent with whom we say we are—that's double-mindedness. In other words, our thoughts (the root and basis of our actions) must please God, not simply our actions alone. It is possible to mask or to impersonate our true thoughts, ideas, intentions and even ourselves by rendering actions that would cause others to perceive us in a certain way, but God knows what we think, knows who we are, and is not confused by mixed messages.

As a man thinketh in his heart, so is he. God knows what we think about Him. So if we are double-minded (in the sense that we say we think one thing, but we think another) then we are unstable and God can't trust us. Let's be diligent to guard our thoughts, minds, and what we allow to exist in our minds. We have the authority and the power to immediately shutdown the thoughts that do not glorify God—as if they were toxic, as if they were cancerous, because they are. They are poisonous and they cannot live.

It doesn't matter whether these thoughts are about people, about how to do things, or about how not to do things—it all refers back to the way we think about God. You see, when we acknowledge that God is in control of all things and that above Him there is none other, our thoughts will be those that promote Him, His way and His will.

"A double minded man is unstable in all his ways." James 1:8 (KJV)

Your Reflections

I had to admit I was wrong when...

That's Impossible!

This is yet a season of miracles. Expect to witness an increase in the unusual, awe-inspiring, breath-taking miracles and moves of God. When miracle after miracle after miracle begin to populate the earth, as the Word and Will of God are confirmed and made manifest before ALL flesh, ALL flesh shall see His mighty works, and God's Name will be Glorified. The dead will rise, the sick will totally recover, the perishing will be rescued, and the weak will be made strong.

Meanwhile, every believer has also entered a season of exceptional grace and favor—Rejoice! For in this season of miracles AND grace AND favor the monumental impossibility and magnitude of your very situation, circumstance, failure and pain has qualified you to participate at an entirely different level and for an entirely different benefit: You shall SEE GOD.

The true essence of a miracle is that it originates and resides outside the auspices and confines of human ability, human logic, and earthly possibility. Miracles are executed exclusively by the Hand, the power and the will of the Almighty God, minus the compromise of human intervention.

All glory, all praise, every credit, and every accolade goes to God. There is a humbling that occurs within us as God simply performs that over which we have no control, input, influence, power or ability to perform—a miracle.

I want to encourage you that your impasse of impossibility is a personal invitation for you to SEE GOD from the vantage point of inside your miracle—that is, outside of the auspices and confines of human ability, human logic, and earthly possibility. God has honored you with an invite and you will honor Him with an RSVP. And how do you RSVP to God? By trusting Him.

Did you know that God has already engineered your precise, personal path in the sea that nobody else can or shall walk in besides you? It must be revealed, because your situation is not simply colored with impossibility—it is ALTOGETHER impossible (with men). But with God, all things are possible! Now that's a good place to hang your faith, renew your hope, and build your expectation. That's a good place to rustle around in your garment of praise. That's a good place to deny and defy every earthly fear and response that your circumstances are demanding of you. That's a good place to trust God—for this is yet a season of miracles.

"Thus says the LORD, who makes a way in the sea And a path through the mighty waters..." Isaiah 43:16 (NKJV)

"But Jesus looked at them and said to them, "With men this is impossible, but with God all things are possible."" Matthew 19:26 (NKJV)

Your Reflections

After today's reading, I am thinking...

Have You Lost Your Mind?

Recently, while driving in an unfamiliar city to an unfamiliar destination, the navigation system in my vehicle instructed me to make a left-turn that I immediately resisted. Tom-Tom Navigation was leading me straight into the entrance of a state mental health facility. When I didn't make the turn, it corrected itself and re-routed me to my destination without fail, but not before I got a good laugh and told Tom-Tom that I had not lost my mind! That's when the Holy Spirit said: Have you lost your mind? I smiled, because I immediately knew the answer. In this season, not only is God demanding that we lose our minds, but He is demanding that we lose our minds boldly and intentionally.

In other words, as we entirely embrace (do not resist) the turns, the adjustments, the assignments, the decisions and the destinies that flag us as being completely under the influence of an Almighty God (no longer under own control), entire destinies will be re-routed just to establish, to demonstrate and to flow into a more perfect measure of faith in God and Kingdom-mindedness. As strongholds of confinement are shattered, there are treasures of knowledge and power that God will release to an "All Sold Out" people.

Don't just drive by. Make a turn to take on the mind of Christ and let Him position you deeper into His Glory, His holiness, and His perfected will. Have you lost your mind?

"But the natural man does not receive the things of the Spirit of God, for they are foolishness to him; nor can he know them, because they are spiritually discerned. But he who is spiritual judges all things, yet he himself is rightly judged by no one. For 'who has known the mind of the LORD that he may instruct Him?' But we have the mind of Christ." 1 Corinthians 2:14-16 (NKJV)

Your Reflections

I have noticed some changes in the way I think about...

Doing the Right Thing

'Doing the right thing' without having the right relationship with God and therefore demonstrating that right relationship with others, does not accomplish what 'doing the right thing' was supposed to accomplish. It negates what God has said when we don't make full use of what (all) He has given us to deliver and to apply HIS correction wherever needed.

The primary goal of forgiveness is to bring us back into right position and relationship with God. It is not to bring us back into the right position with a person, for when we sin, we sin only against God—even if our behavior is towards another. When we forgive without also understanding that it is God's way and God's love that are the governing standards for our lives, our forgiving will only amount to doing the right thing. Yes, we've 'forgiven' the person, but God's governing standard of love cannot produce in us what it was supposed to produce unless and until we forgive because of our relationship and our love for God.

Every benefit of forgiveness comes from God. Let's realize this and 'do the right thing' because we really love Him.

"For those who live according to the flesh set their minds on the things of the flesh, but those who live according to the Spirit, the things of the Spirit. For to be carnally minded is death, but to be spiritually minded is life and peace." Romans 8:5-6 (NKJV)

Your Reflections

Today, I choose to forgive
_____for_____...

The Resources and The Goal

What God has for us in this season is going to require our full attention and our employing all of our resources so that we can fully receive. We see what God has for us. We desire it. We understand it. We have access to it. Yet, unless we move forward intentionally and with all wheels on the ground we will not be able to fully embrace it.

Would anyone accept an offer to drive a car that was missing a steering wheel, a seat or a braking system and then expect the best possible outcome? Absolutely not. Likewise, there is no resource that deserves to be ignored, muffled or abandoned at this time. Locate, inventory, and utilize every resource necessary to fully do what God would have you do.

That which is required of us is of God's doing. The blessing and favor on our lives so structured and ordered by God that it will require an indication of our agreement and our willingness to allow Him to lead us. The actual goal is for us to know and honor God for Who He really is!

It is God's mercy that what He is giving us at this time requires everything we have. Changes must be made in order to get back to what God has said. If it means leaving a job, it is with the assurance that God will provide another way. All our energy and all our resources must be used to do what God has called us to.

The use of your energy, even for something that appears to be right and good, will not yield the favor and the blessing of the Lord as it should if you are not in place. There are those that are waiting for you to be in place so that they can be blessed. You have been so instructed, so ordained, and so assigned by God. Use all of your resources to go toward God.

"as His divine power has given to us all things that pertain to life and godliness," 2 Peter 1:3a (NKJV)

Your Reflections

In which area of your life are you experiencing "Divine Power"?

The Solution

Use everything you have (every resource and every ounce of your energy) to press toward God. What you need in this season is IN God's ways, IN God's principles, IN God's ideas, IN what God is saying to you. You have no time to lose, no energy to misuse or abuse, and no resources to neglect. Use everything you have to press toward God. For in doing so, you will reach what heretofore was unreachable and unsolvable.

The solution is in God. Reach for it. Use every bit of your energy to stretch toward it. Don't say that it's too much or that you cannot do it. You have been given everything you need to operate in the fullest ability to reach the things of God. God would not set a goal before you and then not give you the ability to reach it. You must use your resources plus stretch and challenge yourself to use everything (all) that you have to gain what God has already provided for you. Therein lies the answers, the solutions and the ends of the issues — it is in using everything that you have.

In this season where there are such miracles and such favor, there is also great struggle. So everything you have is going to be needed to reach what God has, to maintain where you are, and to never go back.

"I press toward the mark for the prize of the high calling of God in Christ Jesus." Philippians 3:14 (KJV)

Your Reflections

How would you convince your friend that he/she should try God's way to resolve a problem?

Stay In the Change

Some things never change. It almost seems that your praying for them to change is really a waste of your time — because they haven't changed. Years later when you encounter some people, you realize that they have not changed. Maybe they've changed on the outside, but fundamentally and in terms of principles, they have not changed. So I hear the Lord distinctively saying, "If that which you have prayed would change has not changed, then YOU need to change concerning that thing so that it (things) can change for you."

I had the wonderful occasion of spending time with someone that I had not been around in a long time. It was only a short time before I realized the things that had been irritating to me about that person were still the same. But I made a choice, by the Grace of God, to respond differently to that person's behavior, actions and more specifically their words which were the source of great frustration in times past. I realized that although the person had not changed, I had changed. I had to make a conscious decision not to return to where I used to be even though the person was still there.

God's Grace is available to us to maintain the shift and the change that He has afforded us even when we are confronted with old stimuli. Choose to remain changed. Choose to allow the change that God has given you — whether last week, last month or last year — to remain. Choose to stay in the change so that God's will can be done and God's ways can be seen. You will be able to conduct yourself in the Glory of God and at the end, God gets all the praise.

"Choose my instruction instead of silver, knowledge rather than choice gold," Proverbs 8:10 (NIV)

Your Reflections

Life is so different since I decided to....

New Mercies, New Commitments

The promise of a fresh delivery of new mercies every 24-hours is a great promise to live by. It brings great joy and it brings great hope when you know that if you can make it through these 24-hours, there are streams of mercies you've never known already promised, poised and reserved with your name on them. Be assured that the new mercies are necessary in that either they address new issues or they present another way and another opportunity to address an old issue.

You cannot address the old issues with the old mercies. The real fact of the matter is that if the old mercies were going to help the old issues, then the old issues would not still be an issue in the new day. God gives us new mercies that deal with new issues or that provide a new approach to an old issue. It requires a measure of maturity in God to determine what the new mercies are really for and the bottom line is this: the new mercies equal new commitments.

The new mercies are confirmation that God is speaking, that God is drawing, that God is compelling you to do something new — something that is not rooted and grounded in what you did before. Something that is totally different from the way you previously thought or responded. What is so amazing is that it happens every 24-hours. Morning by morning, new mercies I see — which is an indicator of three things:

1. God's intention is to let us know that He is in control of the day. He is in control of the times and the seasons.

2. God provides a way of escape for every situation we find ourselves in — everyday.

3. God expects us to commit ourselves to that which He has committed Himself to: The success of our day in Him. Why else would He provide new mercies?

So, morning-by-morning, while we're thanking God for the new mercies, we ought to re-commit to His intention for our lives and begin to understand what those re-commitments look like. It may just mean 'get up, take up your bed and walk' instead of lying there with your new mercies and doing nothing with them.

"Jesus said to him, "Rise, take up your bed and walk." John 5:8 (NKJV)

Your Reflections

I experienced a new mercy when...

New Mercies, New Opportunities

We are always excited about the possibilities that a new year holds. We exit the former year thanking God for all He has done and also celebrate entering into the New Year with the hope and faith that things will be new and different. There is, however, one truth that gently pushes our celebration of what is possible in the New Year. It is this: unless you genuinely change the way you do things (which requires a genuine change in yourself—your attitudes, ideas, perspectives, and thoughts), then it is quite possible that nothing at all will change except the date.

The saying 'new day, same story' may seem awfully pessimistic, but in reality that is the truth for those of us who will not embrace the understanding that the best way for us to participate in the new day is to change the way we approach and address issues. I believe we break the heart of God when day in and day out we ignore the opportunities He gives us to change. While we celebrate, morning by morning, new mercies we see, one of those mercies is that we have the opportunity to change—that day! It does not matter how long we have been locked into a particular situation, with the brand new mercies come brand new opportunities to change— that day!

So, embrace every opportunity to start the new day AS A NEW DAY. Ask God what to do and how to do it—for that is when change really comes. We will be required to do some of the same things that we did last year, but the opportunity we have now will be to do it in a way that God's Name is glorified, that God's Will is declared, that God's Love is shown, and that God's intentions and purposes are manifest in the earth realm.

Do we really want to change? If so, it is possible. Only one way: through Jesus Christ, His Love, His Will, His Power and His Grace resting on our lives.

"When Jesus saw him lying there and learned that he had been in this condition for a long time, he asked him, "Do you want to get well?" John 5:6 (NIV)

Your Reflections

Is there an illness (situation) that you have become comfortable with?

Fully Engaged

Make full use of every tool and resource that is available to you during this season of miracles and favor. They may be old, well-used, ignored or forgotten, but everything that God has given you must be used. Your thoughts, concepts, resources, abilities, etc., all need to be fully engaged and operating at full capacity/use in this season of miracles, for they have been given for such a time as this. If you can sing, sing for the miracle—and sing until the miracle is manifest. If you can encourage, encourage for the miracle—and encourage until the miracle is manifest. If you can build, build for the miracle—and build until the miracle is manifest. Whatever you can do, submit it to God, and DO IT.

Your gifts, your abilities, and your resources are primed and ready to be employed for the Kingdom. God is using everything and everyone to show His Glory and to produce His miracle.

"Now there were set there six waterpots of stone, according to the manner of purification of the Jews, containing twenty or thirty gallons apiece. Jesus said to them, "Fill the waterpots with water." And they filled them up to the brim. And He said to them, "Draw some out now, and take it to the master of the feast." And they took it." John 2:6-8 (NKJV)

Your Reflections

Tell of three miracles that have recently occurred.

Fellowship, Friendship, and Relationship

One of the great gifts that God has given to us is the ability to interact with one another. That is, to foster friendships and to fellowship with one other so as to glean of His will and character in each other. Clear demonstrations of God's gifts and His intention for our lives are to be found in the people around us. He intends for us to love one another. He intends for us to gain wisdom and insight about Him from one another.

Many times when we want to know how God operates, we need to look at how He relates our lives to other people, especially when the connection is unlikely. The life of someone we see or touch can be a demonstration of Who God is. We need to look at the relationships we have and begin to perceive how God is demonstrating His will. We 'see God' as we honor His display of Himself in the people around us and through our relationships.

Most people do not desire more 'things' as much as they desire more of us, more of someone to love them and authentic relationship. Even if disappointment is the order of the day, when love is factored in, it doesn't seem so unbearable. Love and relationship make those things that are agonizing (sickness, death, etc.) bearable. With the love of someone else, you can endure.

Fellowship, friendship, and relationship are indeed God's gifts to us. Let's not abuse them.

"And let us consider and give attentive, continuous care to watching over one another, studying how we may stir up (stimulate and incite) to love and helpful deeds and noble activities..." Hebrews 10:24 (AMP)

Your Reflections

Name at least two relationships that need healing in your life. What is your plan for accomplishing that healing?

Seasons of Miracles!

Expect a miracle. Factor God's miracle-working power into your everyday life and thoughts for surely HE IS A GOD OF MIRACLES. Thank God for His miracle-working power in your life and in the lives of those you love. I wonder what life would be like with no miracles... There would be no life, for life itself is a miracle. There would be no salvation... because salvation is a miracle; no healings, no manifestations of dreams and visions, no reconciliation... all these realities fall in the "miracle" category. With every breath and every thought we should thank God for the very abilities that we take for granted are miracles. Just the ability to imagine is a miracle. Yes, these everyday activities are the result of God's miracle working power at work in us. Thank God we don't have to live without them.

One of His greatest miracles is that He allowed a young girl to be the bearer of Glory and then deliver that Glory into the earth in the form of a little baby. That baby, long story short, was the manifestation of God's love in human form. As if that were not enough, He died for our sins, providing a way out of death and hell. Miracles always make other miracles possible.

Just think about it, the miracles that brought Jesus into the earth enabled the miracles that we are experiencing right now. If that virgin had not miraculously conceived and given birth to the Baby, you and I would be bound by sin forever. Thank God.

Peace be with you in the most powerful way, and that is through Jesus Christ, our Lord. God Bless You

"For unto us a Child is born, Unto us a Son is given; And the government will be upon His shoulder. And His name will be called Wonderful, Counselor, Mighty God, Everlasting Father, Prince of Peace. Of the increase of His government and peace There will be no end, Upon the throne of David and over His kingdom, To order it and establish it with judgment and justice.

From that time forward, even forever. The zeal of the Lord of hosts will perform this." Isaiah 9:6-7 (NKJV)

Your Reflections

What miracles can I thank God for today?

A 'Red Room' Response

New responses are necessary for the new thing that God is doing. So consider unfamiliar responses as part of what is new in order for you to completely benefit from the new thing that God has done. If we continue to require the same responses, then there is a great possibility that we will miss the meaning of the new thing that God is doing. In other words, when you respond to God in a new way, with a new attitude, or with a new perspective, and those around you do not respond to you in the way you expect them to respond, don't be amazed. That is proof that they have not yet responded to the new thing in the same way that you have.

The new way, the new thing, the new perspective requires a thought process that shifts you out of the way you used to do things and into the way God desires for you to do the new things. Remember, new is new — it is not rearranged. It is not glossed over. It is not painted. It is totally new.

When a room is painted, it looks new, but it is really the same room. It is your perspectives — therefore your responses — that become new. Your response to a red room might be to trim it with white or other complementary colors. Likewise, a blue room would initiate responses in-line with blue and that color perspective. Your responses will change based on the information presented. To consistently respond exactly the same way 'no matter what color the room,' means it is possible that your perception is off, distorted, or skewed.

When response matches perception it always makes sense.

So when you change your response to God and then people don't respond to you the same old way, that is an indication that you are new — and that is a good thing. When we decide pray an impromptu prayer in response to God, someone will be blessed. When we decide to change our attitude towards someone and to love them in spite of their behavior, then we are blessed and God is pleased. When we decide to honor God (right then and right there) by changing our response to Him, then we are blessed and God is pleased.

"And do not be conformed to this world, but be transformed by the renewing of your mind, that you may prove what is that good and acceptable and perfect will of God." Romans 12:2 (NKJV)

Your Reflections

What challenges do we face while trying to live "the transformed" life?

A Thin Line

There is a very thin line between truth, tradition, and error. Those thin lines need to be regarded and considered carefully. Do not believe everything you hear, everything you see, or even those things you have trusted from year to year without examining their meaning—they all need to be looked at and explored carefully now. I know you don't want to. I know it is much easier to simply accept things the way they have been rather than delve into what they really mean and to then realize that what you believe and what 'you've always done' conflicts with what you understand the Word of God to be saying.

These things do demand our attention. For in our love for God and our desire to do what God has called us to do, we must be diligent to examine ourselves, what we believe, and the implications of what we say and do. The resulting actions, attitudes and thoughts are charged to our account. As leaders in the Body of Christ (and we are all leaders as we live and breathe) we must be careful how we live, which makes a statement about what we believe, who we are, and most of all what we believe about God.

So in this season of traditions when we do lots of what we do 'just because we do,' make sure you make a distinction between those things that are many times all lumped together. In "doing our thing", we do not depend on or look to what fate allows, but we celebrate that God is in control of all things.

"The way of a fool is right in his own eyes, But he who heeds counsel is wise." Proverbs 12:15 (NKJV)

Your Reflections

Traditions are so commonplace; name some your family traditions? What significance do they hold for you?

Light & Revelation

Light and darkness cannot mix. As immediately as light comes, darkness is overcome. Darkness is shattered upon the introduction of light. Once you receive the new revelation, you do not have to revert to the old revelation. The reception of the new revelation simply means that there is no longer a place or use for the old revelation. Now, the old revelation was good in its place and it accomplished what it could. But the new revelation is for the new day, is for the new time, is for the new assignment and cannot be dismissed or ignored as if the old revelation will still work.

Even if you try to retrofit the old revelation and make it still work, you will be sorely, sorely disappointed. Understand that the new revelation is the only way that you can now operate in the perfected will of God. The old has gone, the new has come—embrace the new.

Just like when you wake up each day you don't attempt to travel back into yesterday. No, you accept the new day and proceed to live in it. God is releasing new revelation for His will to be done in your life. It is not that He wants to force it upon you. You need to embrace it and receive it as a demonstration of God's will and testament that He decided for you to live today and to live out His will. 'Thank You' ought to be the response. And then: God, how can I do this most effectively, efficiently, and so that Your Name gets the glory?

It is in your response and in asking those questions that God's perfect will shall be done, that you will have peace, that the Kingdom of God shall be edified, and the Name of Jesus will be glorified. This we do in the Name of Jesus.

"Through the LORD's mercies we are not consumed, because His compassions fail not. They are new every morning; Great is Your faithfulness." Lamentations 3:22-23 (NKJV)

Your Reflections

What will you do today that can be labeled "radically different"?

An Uncommon Glory

I AM filling you with a glory that is uncommon. I AM filling you with a presence that is strange (peculiar out; of the ordinary). I AM filling you with a desire that is pushing you beyond what you have already done. I AM calling forth praise out of you that you have not given. I AM calling you to a place of great grace and there you will find pleasure and peace. It is a wide open place where you will find the spaciousness to love Me, serve Me, hear Me, and know Me in new ways. It is a good place because it is a place that I HAVE established for you. I AM drawing a new praise out of you. I AM drawing out of you a new revelation of the praise that you have already given. It is not because I AM new, it is not because you are new, but it is because I AM doing a new thing in you. However, it is not the new thing that makes the difference: it is your recognition and response to the new thing that really moves you into what I desire for you.

So accept the new, receive the new, and rejoice in the new. This is the new thing that I AM doing in you. [Thus Saith The Lord, Our God]

"Behold, I will do a new thing, Now it shall spring forth; Shall you not know it? I will even make a road in the wilderness And rivers in the desert." Isaiah 43:19 (NKJV)

Your Reflections

Can you change a routine action today? If so, what did you discover?

Sooner, Rather Than Later

Sooner, rather than later, things will happen. They will have already occurred. Submitting those things to God ensures that the journey will be far easier and that the outcomes are of greater value than what you could have anticipated.

I woke up this morning feeling the challenge of the schedule ahead of me for the day. But here I am at three-thirty in the afternoon, having accomplished three-quarters of what was an almost overwhelming challenge and what took most of my attention at seven o'clock this morning. I am alive and well, God has blessed, I have had the opportunity to share of His Glory, I have had the opportunity to minister, I have had the opportunity to go to work and produce income, I have loved someone, I have shown compassion, and I have received compassion from another. ALL of this occurred within the slice of time that beforehand appeared to be a challenge and a struggle for me this morning.

We really need to know that God knows what He is doing and that time is in His Hands. Everything will happen within its time. Because our lives are in God's hands, we shouldn't worry about how things will be orchestrated because they really are in His Hands.

Greet each day praising God and glorifying Him. Seek God's Face in all things. Seek to glorify Him in all things. Then we can be certain that at the end of the day the journey was far easier and the outcomes are of greater value than what we could have anticipated.

"And he shall be like a tree planted by the rivers of water, that bringeth forth his fruit in his season; his leaf also shall not wither; and whatsoever he doeth shall prosper". Psalm 1:3 (KJV)

Your Reflections

What are some of the things that had the power to uproot you? Declare victory over those things right now.

Think New, Be New

There is always something new to learn. There is always a new perspective to consider. There are always new contexts that are presented that bring new revelation — all of which are worthy of consideration all the time. Our minds are always able to comprehend new things even when the exercise of that comprehension is unpleasant or uncomfortable.

There is always the opportunity to think in a new way and therefore to operate in a new way. The acceptance and the reception of those new ideas and thoughts are always dependent upon understanding purpose, destiny and assignment. So it is quite feasible that one who does not understand purpose, does not understand destiny, and does not understand his or her assignment would ignore the new perspective simply because it is not familiar.

It is the presentation of new perspectives, new ideas and new thoughts that begin to shape and re-shape our understanding of the magnificence, magnanimousness, significance and greatness of God. Just when we thought understood it all; God brings new revelation for our consideration in order that we might be more effectively used in the Kingdom. Think new, Be new.

The addition of these thoughts and ideas does not negate what you already know (what God has already revealed), but I am sure that it is God's way of helping us to grow to be able to be more effective conduits so that His Glory gets into the earth realm and that His Kingdom comes on earth even as it is in Heaven.

"Set your mind on things above, not on things on the earth."
Colossians 3:2 (NASB)

Your Reflections

What changes can you make today?

I AM Your God

This is a message to the youth: I AM your God and I have equipped you to do My will in the earth realm, not necessarily to follow the pattern of those you have seen and known—even those that seemed to have "worked well." I AM no longer in the "working well", I AM in relationship. And so I call upon you; you who have much energy, strength, many ideas and various connections that are yet to be made, and those of you who have such a great future before you. I AM calling you. I want a relationship with you that is not built on what you've seen and known, but what I AM doing and the reality of My love for you. I desire that you would know Me. And many shall come to know me! And many shall see My Face and be able to recognize Me as that which they have not seen before and which is unlike anything they've ever known. Thereby you shall know Me as God. For I AM not common. I AM not like everything else and cannot be compared to everything else. Everything else pales in comparison against My Glory. Everything else is weak. Everything else is wimpy. For I AM GOD.

Get to know me. You have a long life ahead of you and not only will you need Me, but you will enjoy Me. You will enjoy My presence and life. You will enjoy worshipping Me. So I come to you as I have come to your fathers and your mothers in times past. I come to you and present Myself to you: Your God, your Strength, your Might, your Wisdom, your Favor, and your Joy. I AM your God and I want your whole heart. [Thus Saith the Lord, Our God] Answer the call.

"Speak to the children of Israel, and say to them: "I am the LORD your God."" Leviticus 18:2 (NKJV)

Your Reflections

Write a description of God.

Now We Can Work Together

Now we can work this thing out: If you let Me work through you and you let your work reflect Me, then everybody looking at you will really see Me, and when they see Me they will understand that it is not you they see, but Me, and they will be drawn to you because I AM in you. Sounds like a riddle, but after all, that is the way life in Christ is. Sounds like something worthy of repeating, like something you've got to hear again, but after all, that is the way life in Christ is. At first glance it doesn't seem to make sense, but it sure works. It brings about My will.

Stop resorting to your own ways. Discouragement has been bound up, disappointment has been cast back into the pit, anguish and anxiety have been overcome by the blood of the Lamb, now walk in the understanding and the confidence that I AM your God and now we can work together.

I know you've read it, but I'll say it you again: If you will be My people, then I WILL be your God. Being your God means that I AM in control of all things, far and near, that concern you. Being your God means that I know what you don't and you can trust Me to work on your behalf—even when you can't figure it out. Being your God means you can let down your defenses and trust Me to take care of these things for you. And, when it is all said and done, you will figure out that it wasn't you, or your witty inventions, or your abilities, but you will be able to say, "THAT was God." [Thus Saith the Lord, Our God]

"For I am the LORD your God, The Holy One of Israel, your Savior; I gave Egypt for your ransom, Ethiopia and Seba in your place." Isaiah 43:3 (NKJV)

Your Reflections

Write a poem or some lyrics that could be a worship song.

My Love is Extravagant

Please remember how much I love you. Remember that My love is not a love that you have experienced, even on your best day, from any human being. My love is divine; it causes divine power and favor to rest upon you. My love is a different kind of love. Please don't compare it to or place a requirement upon it to be like human love. My love is extravagant. My love is purposeful. My love brings transformation. My love stabilizes. My love feeds. My love corrects. My love delivers. My love maintains and holds. My love gives and keeps perspective. My love does what no other love can do, so I need you to treat My love as a different kind of love.

Now I understand that since you are so accustomed to human love, which fails and falls short, it is hard to receive My love and that sometimes you really want Me to prove that I love you. But if you will just accept the fact that I love you, then the resultant relationship between you and Me would cause even more love to be generated. I know that it is not possible for Me to love you any more than I already do, but certainly your eyes would be opened to a greater level of My love.

Please understand just how costly My love is. I sent My Son to die for you and then I raised Him up to live for you, so that you could live for Me.
I LOVE YOU,

Your Heavenly Father

"But God commendeth his love toward us, in that, while we were yet sinners, Christ died for us." Romans 5:8 (KJV)

Your Reflections

Can human love be extravagant? Please explain.

The Word of God is the Standard

It is clear in the scriptures that daily examination of oneself is absolutely necessary for maintaining the right perspective according to the Word of God and therefore, the right behaviors and responses that glorify God. As you examine yourself, be entirely certain that you are using the Word of God as the standard against which you regulate and appraise your standards and principles. It is easy to create your own standards or to use standards that have worked in the past to gauge and measure progress and success in the things of God; however it is ONLY the Word of God that can be used as a proper gauge.

Let's look at it this way: if the goal is to not smoke, and I cut down from smoking five packs a day to three packs a day, while there is reward in reducing from five to three packs a day, the REAL issue is that I shouldn't be smoking at all. So am I to accept my 'cutting down' evaluation as valid? Or should I just not be smoking at all and agree that smoking at any point is not reaching the goal?

Clearly a progression toward the goal is a good thing, but it is not reaching the goal — just like being three blocks away from home is not being home.

It is in this context that that we must begin to ask God for clear revelation, and clarity of understanding and wisdom to know exactly what it is that He is calling us to, and not get inches away and think that we've reached the goal. The best thing is this: God will supply the grace, the favor, the power, the ability, and the anointing that is needed to do what He has called us to do with excellence and perfection — ninety-nine and one-half really just won't do.

"For though I might desire to boast, I will not be a fool; for I will speak the truth. But I refrain, lest anyone should think of me above what he sees me to be or hears from me." 2 Corinthians 12:6 (NKJV)

Your Reflections

What habit have you overcome and how did you do it?

Stand Still and See the Salvation of God

Order your steps and be careful of how you walk and where you go. Be careful of what you are doing and what you are saying, for God is in the midst of everything. Therefore, if we are not careful, we will miss the messages, the methods, and the impartation. But more than that, we will miss the Glory of being connected to an Almighty, Powerful, Magnificent, Loving, and Compassionate God, Who has a plan for our lives. So watch your steps, watch your decisions, watch everything you do and make sure that you are doing as God has instructed you to do.

It is most crucial in this hour, not just for you to benefit and not merely for miracles to come, but so that you can feel the power and the grace to handle God in your life and to know that He is yours and you are His. These decisions will bring you out and into a place of God's will, God's love, God's joy, and God's power. You will know His hand and decide to never be without it.

"The steps of a good man are ordered by the LORD, And He delights in his way." Psalm 37:23 (NKJV)

Your Reflections

Looking back, can you remember a specific time that God was ordering your steps and you didn't even know it, when did realize that it was God?

Season of Phenomenal Growth

It's really the things we do in the spirit realm that contribute to our growth in God, and cause us to reap the fruit benefit of the promises of God. Many believe that they are privileged to not have to do anything and yet prosper in the Kingdom. However, there must be an exercising of your spiritual muscles, that is, your spiritual capacity to facilitate an increase in the manifestation of the simple joys that God has given us access to.

This is a season when those who desire to grow in God are going to do so in great measure, with great speed, and with phenomenal results. Those who refuse to "keep up" (who decline to put in the necessary work and effort) will stand by idly and watch God move through people who they thought would not make it, but who understand the necessity of exercising for spiritual growth. Your prayer life will yield great results when you are consistent with fervent prayer. Your witnessing will yield souls for Jesus when your lifestyle reflects God's love. Your Godly love for people will produce an atmosphere of glory and peace.

You must do something. You must get up. You must try. You must set goals and accomplish them step by step and one by one: Goals that promote the principles of God; Goals that take the reproach off the people of God; and goals that establish the will of God.

"For bodily exercise profits a little, but godliness is profitable for all things, having promise of the life that now is and of that which is to come." 1 Timothy 4:8 (NKJV)

Your Reflections

When I think about "exercises in godliness" these things come to mind…

Keep Growing in Christ

To the faithful believer: resist the temptation to remain stagnant in Christ. You must never stop growing, for there is much danger in reaching a point of stagnation that will not allow you to move on in Christ. The church has suggested that we reach a point, a pinnacle, called "there" that is church prescribed, church approved, and actually means we have arrived. Generally it happens immediately prior to an assignment in ministry that is viewed as the reward. If the reward is a position in an ever-growing church, then at the very least, one is required to keep up with the corporate growth.

This requires growing and stretching personally, so that you're not left behind as the corporate flow comes. Revival has come and we must be mature enough to handle revival in ourselves and in the land. Let us move on to maturity.

"let us go on to perfection, not laying again the foundation of repentance from dead works and of faith toward God." Hebrews 6:1b (NKJV)

Your Reflections

How is your church helping you to grow?

Pure in Heart

God is looking for the restoration of the desire for purity. A pure heart has one focus. It is committed to the focus maintaining its place and also to the goal of the focus. Sadly, in the world in which we live today, we have arrived at the place where ambiguity is acceptable. However, ambiguity is an enemy of the standard of holiness, an enemy of the lifestyle and the character of God, an enemy to our own one-mindedness. This becomes a welcome mat to compromise, complacency, and the acceptance of things that are against (have nothing to do with) the will of God.

So decide for yourself who you will serve, how you will do it, and with whom you will unite your heart and mind with in order to get it done — and then focus on that alone, so that you don't fall prey to an ambiguous spirit that says it's okay to do it this way today and another way tomorrow.

For in this season, there is a special release, revelation, and blessing for those who will not be deterred by the cares of this world, or what is fashionable, or what is the trend, or what is more of a personal preference rather than a Biblical principle or truth. That blessing is that we shall see the glory of God in great measure. Blessed are the pure in heart, for they shall see God.

Now it isn't the blessing or the miracle that we look to see. Rather, we look to see the very presence and essence of God, Himself. We've gotten used to considering the blessings and the miracles as God, Himself — but they are not. Blessing and the miracles are what God does. But God said He would show Himself directly. We shall SEE God. His principles unfolded, His Word manifested, His Glory come into the earth realm, because we decide to have a singleness of mind and heart.

"Blessed are the pure in heart, For they shall see God." Matthew 5:8 (NKJV)

Your Reflections

What issues threaten the purity of your heart?

Do Not Be Deceived

Receive this strong, compelling entreatment from the mouth of God:
Do not play with My commandments and do not act as though I have not spoken to you. You see things going awry, turning into a complete mess and you suppose that it can't happen to you, but do not be deceived, do not be fooled. Should I lift My favor from you, everything in your life would be in shambles.

Do not play with obedience concerning Me, for you need to understand that half-obedience is not obedience at all. A desire to do right or to be sympathetic to doing what is right, less the action and the follow through of actually doing right, does not accomplish My will. Acting one way today and another way tomorrow, with no consistency, does not please Me.

Excuse-making and compromising, and then looking to Me to forgive arbitrarily is almost in the category of ludicrous. To suppose that you will never have to answer to Me — that I will simply turn my face and not judge what you say and do is not nearly as wise as walking blind-folded on commuter train tracks during rush hour.
Get it together.   [SAITH THE LORD, OUR GOD]

"Your iniquities have turned these things away, And your sins have withheld good from you." Jeremiah 5:25 (NKJV)

"Do not be deceived, God is not mocked; for whatever a man sows, that he will also reap." Galatians 6:7 (NKJV)

Your Reflections

How does this word of wisdom speak to you?

SIN: Light or Darkness

It is amazing how we entertain ungodly desires and then wonder why our lives don't match the façade of holiness that we push. It's plain and simple: light and darkness cannot dwell in the same place. This goes against the grain of many of us (our preferences). Our ears are not used to hearing it, but the fact of the matter is that the wages of sin is death and the gift of God is eternal life. This death is not only physical death, but it is the spiritual death that we live in and shall be our experience when we make deliberate decisions to come against the will of God.

Choose the will of God today and be refreshed.

"But if serving the LORD seems undesirable to you, then choose for yourselves this day whom you will serve, whether the gods your forefathers served beyond the River, or the gods of the Amorites, in whose land you are living. But as for me and my household, we will serve the LORD." Joshua 24:15 (NIV)

"Repent, then, and turn to God, so that your sins may be wiped out, that times of refreshing may come from the Lord," Acts 3:19 (NIV)

Your Reflections

What are your thoughts about sin?

SIN: Vicious Cycle

Sin destroys life. The life that God has given us is destroyed by not only by the intent to sin, but by the actual sin itself. Many of us are ensnared in the vicious cycle of actually planning to sin coupled with an 'insurance policy' of planning to ask God to forgive us.

Then we are bewildered and in complete denial about the reality that we ourselves have created. The vicious cycle causes us to spiral down to a place where hopelessness is our everyday clothing, and where hopelessness lines the room of every place we find ourselves. It is because of sin and the insistence on doing what we desire to do.

If you want your life to come into agreement with God's will, then you must intentionally forgo sin. Opt out. It is not that any of us are going to ever be perfect on this side of heaven. However, the desire to do what is right and to please God by making a choice against the things that don't please Him, yield a measure of joy and peace that are not otherwise possible.

"Now, O Israel, listen to the statutes and the judgments which I teach you to observe, that you may live, and go in and possess the land which the LORD God of your fathers is giving you."
Deuteronomy 4:1 (NKJV)

Your Reflections

Can you recall a time when a cycle of sin dominated your life?

But With God...

Intentionally pursue your dreams. Pursue the impossible. Do not give up on what has not come to pass. IT is possible—it really is. Now the IT is varied and complex. The IT are those things that you've been asking for, that you've been believing God for, and that you've almost given up on. So today, favor is possible. Forgiveness is possible. Freedom from bondage is possible. True liberty is possible. Faith is possible. The sale of property is possible. Moving into your new home is possible. It is possible for your daughter to be healed. It is possible for your entire mind to be at peace. It is possible for you to meet your Mr. or Miss Right.

ALL things are possible with God.

It IS possible that you will get a new job.

It IS possible that you will be able to save some money for a rainy day.

It IS possible that you will have peace.

It IS possible that your blood pressure and blood sugar will be normal.

It IS possible for that tumor to dry up.

It IS possible that you can say 'I love you' to those who have despitefully used you.

It IS possible that you can really be happy and to not be afraid that happiness will be quickly absorbed by pain and tragedy.

It IS possible for you to get into school, excel, and Graduate with honors..

It IS possible. ALL things are possible with God.

Have faith in God.

"But Jesus looked at them and said to them, "With men this is impossible, but with God all things are possible." Matthew 19:26 (NKJV)

Your Reflections

List some possibilities for your life...now makes some declarations for someone else.

I Believe. Final Answer.

In the midst of the Kingdom, there is an inevitable tension and a setting apart that occurs when the believer finally decides to truly believe what God is currently saying through His written Word, through His preached Word, or through His revealed Word (revelation). That tension and setting apart happens because once you really and truly believe, you are changed and you can no longer go back to the things that you used to do.

This might present a problem for those who have become accustomed to relating to you in a specific way — because your responses are expected to be what they have always been. However, once you really believe God, your desire is to do what HIS will is concerning a thing, rather than what you have always done. That desire will most surely thrust you out of and away from what is normative for you and into the 'new' that is already planned for you. And know this: even if new is not comfortable, it is wonderful — so do not resist the tendency, the movement, or the inclination to become new.

When I was growing up they used to say "Oh, you're breaking new on me." What that really meant was this: I was choosing to respond to things differently. I was choosing to act in a different way. I was choosing to demand a different response from others. And you must do just that — break new! For in that newness is the peace, is the power, is the presence that comes from God and the new thing that He is doing.

"I show you specified new things from this time forth, even hidden things [kept in reserve] which you have not known." Isaiah 48:6b (AMP)

Your Reflections

What are some "new" ideas you have been considering?

Let Your Faith Grow!

Dreams and visions that have not come to pass are on the agenda for the next twenty-one days. Dreams and vision that have been a source of frustration for you because you have known what God has said, but you have not seen them come to pass yet, will be released now in a season of increased faith.

So let your faith grow. Let it open up and grow tall, deep, and wide so as to be able to sustain the manifestation of these gifts. Above all, remember God loves you. He is not a man that He should lie, but He is faithful to every promise, every gift, every vision, and every dream that comes from Him—so receive it. Believe it like never before and watch it come to pass.

Your best defense against the weakening of your faith is a godly atmosphere. Worship more, your faith will grow; Pray more, your faith will grow; meditate more, your faith will grow; read the Word of God, your faith will grow; fellowship with other Christians, your faith will grow.

"God is not a man, that he should lie, nor a son of man, that he should change his mind. Does he speak and then not act? Does he promise and not fulfill?" Numbers 23:19 (NIV)

Your Reflections

Construct a plan for your personal growth based on a God-given dream or vision.

Reshaped and Reformed

Ragged, torn, disheveled, unkempt, broken down, and incapacitated is the image that the enemy wants you to have of yourself, your situation, your affairs, and your loved ones.

But instead, I have given you a NEW VISION — a NEW IMAGE. The new vision/image I AM giving you is of one who has worked hard to assemble/develop a new image, new hair color, new makeup, new shades of lipstick, etc. You have worked hard and now must be diligent to not let that image slip up or fade away just because you've stopped working at it or acknowledging it for what it is.

I AM making you new. I AM reshaping and reforming every area of your life. I AM doing it swiftly and without permission from you — for I AM YOUR GOD. [Thus Saith The Lord, Our God]

"He has made everything beautiful in its time. Also He has put eternity in their hearts, except that no one can find out the work that God does from beginning to end." Ecclesiastes 3:11 (NKJV)

Your Reflections

Write a prayer for your reshaping.

An Ecosystem of Advancement

The lions, tigers, bears and all manner of ferocious animals are not meant to scare you. They are meant to remind you of the diversity and complexity of God. They are meant to remind you of how many things God has caused to exist together on the earth. The many kinds of things –animals, birds, people, fish, and insects—all represent the vast and wondrous enormity of our God. He made us all and created us to work together as in an ecosystem. One thing feeds off of the other and in the end, it all works out.

In the spirit realm God is saying the same thing. It is all working out. The things that seem possible, the things that seem impossible, the new things, the old things, the things that are as you never dreamed, the things that you dreamed that are coming to pass—all of it is working together to accomplish God's complete perfected will concerning your life.

So you will have to take the good and the bad, the easily attained and the challenges, and understand that in God's hand all of these tools lose their ability to destroy us. They are fully incapacitated. Instead, they become opportunities and tools for our advance in Him.

"Indeed My hand has laid the foundation of the earth, And My right hand has stretched out the heavens; When I call to them, They stand up together." Isaiah 48:13 (NKJV)

Your Reflections

Name those that are part of your ecosystem of advancement and explain why.

Heightened Perception

Be sure to benefit from this season of the pouring out of My blessings. Be sure to recognize the power you have within your mouth to declare and proclaim the things I have for you. Be sure your words come into agreement with the provision I have for your life. Be sure you do not complain of Me or My ability and thus dull your sensitivity of Me to receive My blessings.

Instead, receive the heightened perception that I have for you. Each moment of each day is a specific, definite, accurate, undeniable, and distinguished blessing. Oh, it may be a little tedious to ponder and consider every moment with such gravity and detail, because even as you are considering them they are going on and on. But please know that whatever I have for you, I have for you. Whatever I have decided is yours, is yours. Nothing shall be able to separate you from My Love. [SAITH THE LORD, OUR GOD]

"For I am persuaded that neither death nor life, neither angels nor principalities nor powers, neither things present nor things to come, neither height nor depth, nor any other created thing, shall be able to separate us from the love of God, which is in Christ Jesus our Lord."
Romans 8:38-39 (MEV)

Your Reflections

Create the verse for a greeting card that would encourage the readers.

They Will Fit Again

I AM restoring the time of lives fitting together...
It is a good thing that you did not throw away the people that
seem to no longer fit in your life because they will fit again.
The fact of the matter is this: they never stopped fitting
because it was part of My divine plan that they were there in
the first place. As you took a turn to the left and as you took a
turn to the right, it seemed that some people just no longer fit.
I AM restoring the time of lives fitting together in ways that I
have declared they would fit.

Now don't be upset that it will become necessary for
you to re-visit your ability to love those who despitefully use
you. Now don't be upset that it will become necessary for you
to disregard your personal preferences to allow My Will to
work in your life. As you do, the blessing that I have for you
will rest upon you with GREAT measure.

So lay aside your personal images and preferences and
receive what I have for you. Otherwise, you will miss the
opportunity that I have for you to live in a measure of wisdom
and understanding that will bring you great peace. [THUS
SAITH THE LORD, OUR GOD]

*"Therefore we also, since we are surrounded by so great a cloud of
witnesses, let us lay aside every weight, and the sin which so easily
ensnares us, and let us run with endurance the race that is set before
us, looking unto Jesus, the author and finisher of our faith, who for
the joy that was set before Him endured the cross, despising the
shame, and has sat down at the right hand of the throne of God."
Hebrews 12:1-2 (NKJV)*

Your Reflections

What does it mean to "throw someone away"? Have you ever thrown someone away? Have you ever been thrown away? Explain what this feels like?

What Time is It?

You must know when it is time to begin fresh and anew, to start over again, to bring to a conclusion what is, to revamp, or to change direction. We must know these things — without fear — and be able to step into them with courage.

In this season, God is providing those with whom you will be able to share and to discuss these things. Whereas in the past, you were not able to discuss them due to fear of misunderstanding or fear that those with whom we shared would seize your thoughts and run ahead of you.

Do not be discouraged. Do not be dismayed. Do not be quiet. No one will be able to do what YOU are called to do in this season. However, you must resist the pull to do things on our own and without the wise counsel and company of anointed men and women around us. For what God is saying to you, He is also saying to others. As a result of our conversations and our relationship with others, we will (together) accomplish the perfected Will of God.

Spend this season in prayer asking for wisdom and revelation, for God is pouring out a new way, new wisdom, new understanding, new methods, and that with new favor that we would receive new joy, have new power and see manifestations of God's Power in the ministries that we are in.

God Bless you and the Peace of God be with you.

"Behold, I will do a new thing, Now it shall spring forth; Shall you not know it? I will even make a road in the wilderness And rivers in the desert." Isaiah 43:19 (NKJV)

Your Reflections

Everybody becomes discouraged at some point, when was that for you? And how did you overcome it?

By The Book

Do it by the Book. As you have been told and as you have been instructed: do it, for there is grace to follow directions that heretofore you have not been able to follow. There is wisdom to understand instructions that you have never been able to understand. There is the blessing of the Lord upon those who seek out God's way, not being satisfied with their own way.

Follow the letter to a T and do it by the Book. In the end, the blessing will be that the perfected will of God put forth for your life, the will of God in which He has promised to operate, and the will of God which He uses to bless you and bring forth miracles, signs, and wonders will follow. Follow by the Book.

You have never been this way before, so do what God says do. You have never been as blessed as you are, so do what God says do. You have never had as much favor as you currently have, so do what God says do. Follow by the Book.

"Yet there shall be a space between you and it, about two thousand cubits by measure. Do not come near it, that you may know the way by which you must go, for you have not passed this way before."
Joshua 3:4 (NKJV)

Your Reflections

Find and list five passages of scripture that are speaking to your current situation.

Desire To Do God's Will

Kindle the fire of the desire to do the will of God in your life. In this season something as simple as agreeing with God and wanting what God wants is so crucial and significant. It does not require knowledge of processes, timelines, purposes, or reasons. It just takes agreement with the fact that God is God and above Him there is not another.

Do everything you can do to agree with God. Make every effort to stand in agreement with God. Make every effort to bring ALL your heart, desires, concerns, preferences, and musings in line with God. There is a blessing in wanting to agree with God. Resist the temptation to reject the truth of God and demand that your life line up with His will.

Knowing you are in agreement with The One who created the earth, yields a measure of peace that cannot be explained.

Agreement with The One who made the earth will yield your ability to bring about what you alone are unable to do. So look for the miracle—just because you agree.

"For in it the righteousness of God is revealed from faith to faith; as it is written, "The just shall live by faith."" Romans 1:17 (NKJV)

Your Reflections

Write ten affirmations for your life from God's Word.

Power In Your Dreams

There is power in your dreams. Those things that you are dreaming, envisioning, and even those things that seem impossible, yet so real, are what God is using in this season to inspire you and keep you focused on what is possible. Focusing on what is actually happening is not conducive to believing for what you cannot see.

God has given us dreams just for this purpose. Set your mind on what you have been dreaming. Begin to think about what is necessary for that dream to be manifest and know that God has not given it to you just to dream it and never experience it.

This is a good time to ask God what steps you need take in order to bring it to pass. This is a good time to ask God what you need to see, where you need to be, and who you need to know to make you dreams come to pass. You can be assured that He will answer. For the dreams God has placed in your head, in your mind, and in your spirit, are His way of assuring you that He knows the plans that He has for you; plans to prosper you and not to harm you; plans to give you a future and a hope.

"And it shall come to pass in the last days, says God, That I will pour out of My Spirit on all flesh; Your sons and your daughters shall prophesy, Your young men shall see visions, Your old men shall dream dreams." Acts 2:17 (NKJV)

Your Reflections

Record some of the dreams and visions that God has given you.

Power Made Perfect In Weakness

Discouragement and disappointment are parts of the plan and the plot of the enemy to switch you into a mode of disobedience. Not just acting in disobedience, but actually assuming a disobedient stand because the things that would make you obedient do not seem to you as if they would relieve your discouragement and disappointment.

Resist every temptation in your spirit to go against what you know is My Will. This great tool of discouragement and disappointment is ruling and reigning, but cannot ultimately rule, for I (God) AM greater in you than any experience, demonstration, or illustration of discouragement or disappointment outside of you. I have put within you a (My) desire to do My Will. When you obey My desire, you are operating in My Strength, which brings forth My Will, yields to the power of the Holy Spirit (who teaches you all things), and causes you to be empowered. For when you are weak, then you are strong.

I know you feel like you can't make it — like you're not going to make it. I know you don't know how you're going to make it. But all those uncertainties are consistent with what the enemy does and how he operates. I SAY: you shall live and not die. I SAY: you are the head and not the tail. I SAY: beloved, I DESIRE that you would prosper and be in good health — even as your soul prospers. And THAT is enough. [Thus Saith The Lord, Our God]

"But he said to me, "My grace is sufficient for you, for my power is made perfect in weakness." Therefore I will boast all the more gladly about my weaknesses, so that Christ's power may rest on me." 2 Corinthians 12:9 (NIV)

Your Reflections

Write ten affirmations for your life from God's Word.

Oh, How I Love You!

This day I say unto you: You are My beloved and there is nothing in this earth that means more to Me than you. I love you. I support you. I encourage you and I accept you — just as you are. So much so that I accept the things about you that you don't even accept about yourself.

I love you with an everlasting love and I AM pushing you toward your destiny and purpose — even without your consent. This brings Me great joy and will also bring joy to you and to those around you.

I enjoy you. I enjoy seeing you enjoy your life. I enjoy knowing that you love Me. I enjoy receiving your worship. Yes, despite your disappointments, pain, discouragement, doubts and fears, you DO bring Me joy — and I delight to love you, to bless you and to make you an open example of My Love.

So, erase the doubt. Throw away the lies of the devil. For you ARE my beloved. I DO love you, and I enjoy being with you. I delight to awaken you each morning so that you can start another day and I can be with you throughout it. Oh, how I love you! And I DO appreciate your love for Me. [Thus Saith the Lord, Our God]

"Who shall separate us from the love of Christ? Shall tribulation, or distress, or persecution, or famine, or nakedness, or peril, or sword? As it is written: "For Your sake we are killed all day long; We are accounted as sheep for the slaughter." Yet in all these things we are more than conquerors through Him who loved us. For I am persuaded that neither death nor life, nor angels nor principalities nor powers, nor things present nor things to come, nor height nor

depth, nor any other created thing, shall be able to separate us from the love of God which is in Christ Jesus our Lord." Romans 8:35-39 (NKJV)

Your Reflections

I am sure of God's love when:

Pray Until Something Happens

It is such an amazing privilege to pray for someone. To actually be used by God to pray for God's will to be manifest in the life of a sister or brother is simply awesome. Just think, God allows us to participate in what He is doing in the earth. Although He doesn't needs to, He depends on us to discern His desires and put our faith into action to bring it to pass. Sometimes God allows us to pray because a friend or family member does not know the power of prayer, but He wants to get a blessing into their life. Sometimes it is a faith issue and God just needs someone with enough faith to ask/agree with Him to get that blessing into the earth realm.

There is the necessity of expectation (faith's first cousin) mixed with the miracle of vision (the ability to see what God wants). Then there is the issue of the development of our faith that God is so committed to. It is good that we have to pray. Praying out of desperation can be beneficial, resulting in a level of prayer not required by casual thoughts and desires. We are admonished in the scripture not to faint, instead pray. And do it until somethings have to manifest.

We get God's attention when we set aside our needs and desires to pick up our sister's concerns, when we place our brother's welfare above our own needs to petition God's intervention.

Somebody is waiting for you to pray for him or her. Somebody needs your faith to rise up to get his or her blessing in the earth. A friend, a co-worker, a neighbor, a colleague, a cousin is waiting for you to go to God on their behalf. And not only you, but also they are waiting for you to gather others to come together to break satan's hold in a situation.

"So Peter was kept in prison, but earnest prayer for him was made to God by the church."

Acts 12:5 ESV

Your Reflections

Call a friend and ask what you can pray about for them, then do it on the spot.

Calling all Sisters:

Join us for Weekly for Study and Conversation

Calling all Brothers:

Join us for Weekly for Study and Conversation

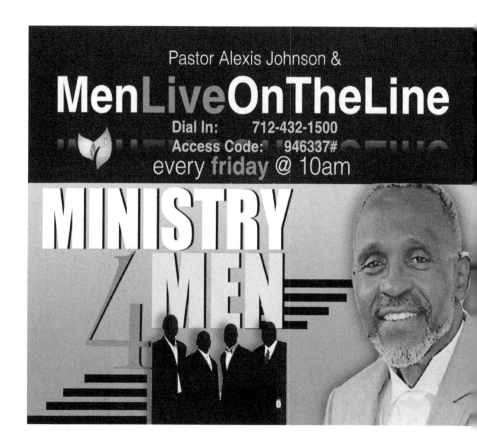

Made in the USA
Middletown, DE
04 March 2019